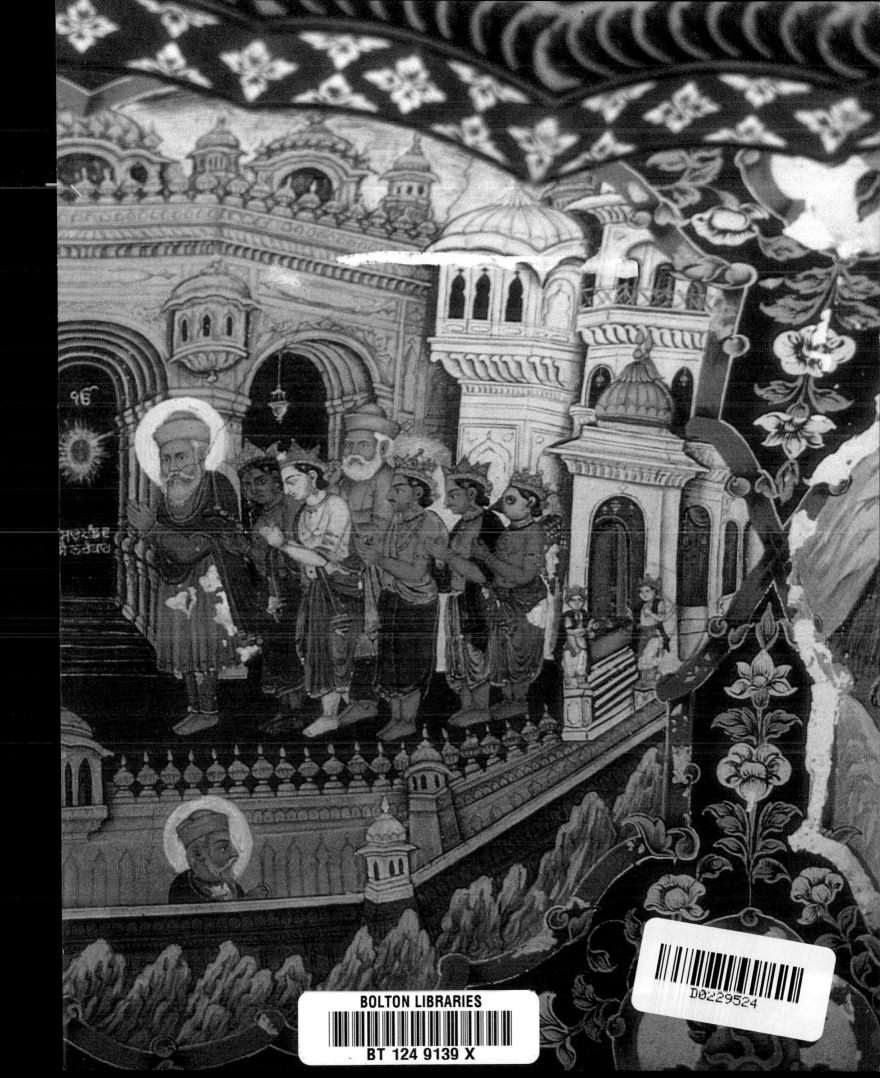

THE
FACTS ABOUT

SIKHISM

Alison Cooper

HODDER
Wayland

an imprint of Hodder Children's Books

This book is based on the original title *Sikhism* by Beryl Dhanjal, in the *What do we know about...?* series, published in 1996 by Macdonald Young Books

This differentiated text version by Alison Cooper, published in 2004 by Hodder Wayland, an imprint of Hodder Children's Books
© Hodder Wayland 2004

Original designer and illustrator: Celia Hart
Layout for this edition: Jane Hawkins
Consultant: Working Group on Sikhs and Education (WORKSE)

Hodder Children's Books
A division of Hodder Headline Limited,
338 Euston Road London NW1 3BH

Photograph acknowledgements: Andes Press Agency, p31(b) (Carlos Reyes Manzo); The British Library, p21(t); Beryl Dhanjal, p16(b); Format Photographers, pp8(I), 24 (Judy Harrison); Hulton Deutsch, p19(b); The Hutchison Library, p27(t); Magnum Photos, pp39(b), 41(t) (Raghu Rai), 41(b) (P Marlow); Bipinchandra J Mistry, endpapers, pp9, 14, 21(b), 23(b), 25(t), 29, 36, 37(t), 37(b); Network Photographers, pp31(t) (Barry Lewis), 33 (Martin Meyer); Christine Osborne Pictures, pp8(r), 26, 32, 34, 43; Ann & Bury Perless, pp13(t), 19(t); Rex Features, p33; Trip, pp12, 13(b), 15(t), 15(b), 16(t), 17, 18, 20, 22, 23(t), 25(b), 27(b), 28, 29, 30, 35(t), 35(b), 38, 39(t) (Suresh Gavali), 40, 42 (Helene Rogers).

Printed and bound by WKT Company Limited

A CIP catalogue record for this book is available from the British Library

ISBN 0 7502 46553

Endpapers: A scene from a wall painting of Guru Nanak's life.

CONTENTS

WHO ARE THE SIKHS?

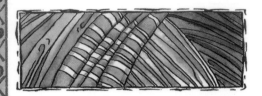

Most Sikh families are from India. Sikhs believe in one God. They follow the teachings of the ten Gurus, who set up the Sikh religion. They read the message of the Gurus in the holy book, the Guru Granth Sahib.

Some Sikhs belong to the Khalsa, a community set up by the tenth Guru. They follow certain rules about how to dress and behave.

◄ The *gurdwara*

The people in the photograph are standing outside their *gurdwara*. The *gurdwara* is the building where the holy book is kept. Sikhs meet there for worship, to share news and to eat together. Being together is very important for Sikhs.

There are no priests at the gurdwara. People called Granthis look after the building and the holy book.

Learning the faith ►

These British children are learning about the Gurus at the *gurdwara*. They are also learning Punjabi, which is the language spoken by Sikhs in India.

Number of gurdwaras
in a country

- Over 100
- 50 to 100
- 10 to 50
- 1 to 10

Sikhs around the world

Most Sikh families are originally from India. There are about 14 million Sikhs in India itself but they make up only two per cent of the population. There are some Sikhs in many other countries, especially Britain, Canada and the USA.

▲ **The Guru Granth Sahib**

The book in the photograph above is the Guru Granth Sahib. Sikhs think of their holy book as their teacher and leader. They treat it with the respect they would give to a human Guru. Each morning they open the book and read the verse at the top of the left-hand page. The words of the Guru Granth Sahib guide them through their day.

 STUDENTS

People who went to hear the teachings of Guru Nanak, the first Guru, were given the name 'Sikhs'. The word *Sikh* means student or learner in Punjabi.

9

TIMELINE

EVENTS IN SIKHISM

1469 Guru Nanak, the founder of Sikhism, is born near Lahore.	**1526** Babur invades India and establishes the Mogul Empire.	**1539** Guru Nanak dies. He has already chosen Guru Angad to take over from him.	**1552** Guru Amar Das becomes Guru. He started the Guru's kitchen.	**1574** Guru Ram Das becomes Guru.	**1577** The city of Amritsar is founded by Guru Ram Das.

Guru Nanak

1849–1947 The British rule Panjab. They improve transport and build schools and hospitals.	**1845–6** **1848–9** Two wars are fought between the Sikhs and the British, who are trying to take over Panjab.	**1839** Ranjit Singh dies.	**1799** Ranjit Singh becomes emperor.	**1700s** Panjab is invaded many times and Sikh leaders also fight each other.	**1707** Aurangzeb, the last great Mogul emperor, dies.
1873 A group of Sikh leaders say that everyone should belong to the Khalsa.					

Ranjit Singh

1890s Many Sikhs move to East Africa to work.	**1919** Sikhs celebrating Vaisakhi in Amritsar are massacred by British soldiers.	**1920** A special committee is set up to take charge of *gurdwaras*.	**1921–1925** There are quarrels over whether *gurdwaras* are owned by individual families or are public property.	**1925** The Sikh Gurdwaras Act in India sets out who is a Sikh and makes a difference between Sikhs and Hindus.	**1947** India becomes independent and a new country, Pakistan, is established. Most Sikhs settle in India.

India divided

India was ruled by Britain from the early 1800s until 1947. When India became independent, a new, separate country called Pakistan was set up for India's Muslims. The border between India and Pakistan ran through the state of Panjab. Most of the Sikhs who lived in Panjab moved to the Indian side of the border. However, the places where the Gurus were born and died were in Pakistan. It became impossible for Sikhs in India to visit these places because relations between India and Pakistan were very bad.

1581 Guru Arjan becomes Guru. He puts together the holy book, the Guru Granth Sahib.	1604 The first copy of the Guru Granth Sahib is placed in the Harmandir at Amritsar.	1606 Guru Arjan dies defending the Sikh faith. Guru Hargovind takes over.	1644 Guru Har Rai becomes Guru.
			1661 Guru Har Krishan becomes Guru when he is only five years old.
1704 The two small sons of Guru Govind Singh are killed for refusing to become Muslims.	1699 The Khalsa is founded.	1675 Guru Govind Singh becomes Guru. He fights many battles.	1664 Guru Har Krishan dies of smallpox and is followed by Guru Teg Bahadar. He is beheaded in Delhi in 1675.
1950s–1960s Many Sikhs move to Britain, the USA, Canada and other countries to look for work.	1966 Punjabi is made the official language in part of Panjab to make sure it does not die out.	1984 Militant Sikhs and the Indian army fight around the Harmandir in Amritsar. The Akal Takhat is badly damaged.	

Sri Guru Granth Sahib

Guru Govind Singh

▲ *Khanda*

The Sikh symbol

The Sikh symbol is called the *khanda*. It is made up of a double-edged sword (also called a *khanda*). The *khanda* is circled by a weapon called a *chakka* and enclosed by two curved swords (*kirpans*) which symbolize the need to be both a soldier and a saint.

HOW DID SIKHISM BEGIN?

The founder of Sikhism was Guru Nanak. He was born in 1469 at Nankana Sahib, which was in north-west India but is now in Pakistan. Many Indians believe that people are reborn over and over again, until they achieve union with God. Sikhs believe that Guru Nanak was a special teacher, who chose to be reborn so that he could help people to find a new way to God. The people who went to hear Guru Nanak teach were the first Sikhs.

◄ Guru Nanak

This is a modern painting of Guru Nanak. When he was a young man, Nanak was devoted to God. One day he disappeared into a river and found himself in God's court. There, he was told to teach people how to follow God's path.

Guru Nanak used poetry to teach people about God. He would sing his poems while his Muslim friend Mardana played music. He taught people that they could avoid being continually reborn if they looked towards God and tried to become part of God. This was something they could achieve during their lives, not after death.

Panjab

The map on the left shows the region of Panjab. The name Panjab means 'five rivers'. Most of the places that are important to Sikhs are in Panjab, including the city of Amritsar and the Harmandir (see page 28).

The Moguls ▶

The people who ruled India during the lives of the ten Sikh Gurus were called the Moguls. The first Mogul ruler was Babur, who invaded India from the north in 1526. This was during Guru Nanak's lifetime. Babur is shown in the centre of the painting on the right.

◀ Guru Nanak's childhood

Most pictures show Guru Nanak as an old man. This picture shows him as a boy, looking after his family's cattle.

MOGUL PRINCES

The Mogul rulers loved painting, music and architecture. One of Babur's descendants built the Taj Mahal, one of the world's most beautiful buildings. But they were sometimes cruel, especially to their enemies.

WHO WERE THE TEN GURUS?

The ten human Gurus were teachers and leaders of the Sikh community. After the first three Gurus, the role of Guru passed from father to son or to other family members. Seven of the Gurus were prophets, who wrote down the message that is in the Guru Granth Sahib. The holy book itself became the Sikhs' teacher when there were no more human Gurus.

The ten Gurus ▶

The poster on the right shows the ten Gurus. The Gurus strengthened the Sikh community. They built towns and temples, provided hospitals and set up a kitchen, so that all the people who came to see them could share a meal together. The fifth Guru, Guru Arjan, and the ninth Guru, Guru Teg Bahadar, were killed for their beliefs.

 OTHER MEANINGS

The word 'Guru' has other meanings, besides human teacher. It means God as people can know Him. It also means the voice of God inside you, or your conscience. Sikhs believe that when they are gathered together, the Guru is there among them.

ੳ ਅ ੲ ਸ ਹ
ਕ ਖ ਗ ਘ ਙ
ਚ ਛ ਜ ਝ ਞ
ਟ ਠ ਡ ਢ ਣ
ਤ ਥ ਦ ਧ ਨ
ਪ ਫ ਬ ਭ ਮ
ਯ ਰ ਲ ਵ ੜ

◀ The alphabet

This alphabet is used to write Gurmukhi, the language of the Guru Granth Sahib.

Miri and Piri ▶

Guru Hargovind sat on a throne between two swords. He said these represented Piri (spiritual power) and Miri (power in the world). The photograph shows two flagpoles called *Miri* and *Piri* in Amritsar, in Panjab.

Offering water ▼

The *gurdwara* in this photograph is built on the spot in Delhi where the eighth Guru, Guru Har Krishan, died. The Sikhs standing outside are offering cool water to people passing by.

WHAT IS THE KHALSA?

The Khalsa is a community of Sikhs that was set up by Guru Govind Singh, the tenth Guru. The Guru taught that members of the Khalsa should love God so much that they thought about nothing else. He told them to wear special signs and follow rules of behaviour to show that they were members of the Khalsa.

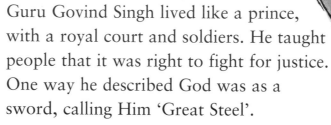

A double-edged sword

◄ Guru Govind Singh

Guru Govind Singh lived like a prince, with a royal court and soldiers. He taught people that it was right to fight for justice. One way he described God was as a sword, calling Him 'Great Steel'.

How the Khalsa was founded ▼

One day Guru Govind Singh told a crowd of Sikhs he wanted the head of one of them. Who was prepared to die? Eventually a man came forward. The Guru took him into a tent and the people outside heard the swish of a sword. Blood flowed out from the tent. The Guru did this five times but then, amazingly, he brought the five men out alive. He called them the Five Beloved Ones. They were the first members of the Khalsa. The story is shown in this carved picture which is from the Harmandir in Amritsar.

The five 'K's ▼

Guru Govind Singh told Sikhs to follow five rules in the way they dressed to show that they were members of the Khalsa. He told them not to cut their hair. He also told them to wear a steel bangle on their right wrist and a special undergarment called *kachh*. They were to carry a comb and a sword with a curved blade. These five signs begin with the letter 'K'.

SIKH NAMES

Men were given the title 'Singh' (meaning 'Lion') when they joined the Khalsa. Women were called 'Kaur', meaning 'Princess'. Today people use these names even if they are not members of the Khalsa. Sikh names can be used for boys or girls, so Amarjit Singh is a boy and Amarjit Kaur is a girl.

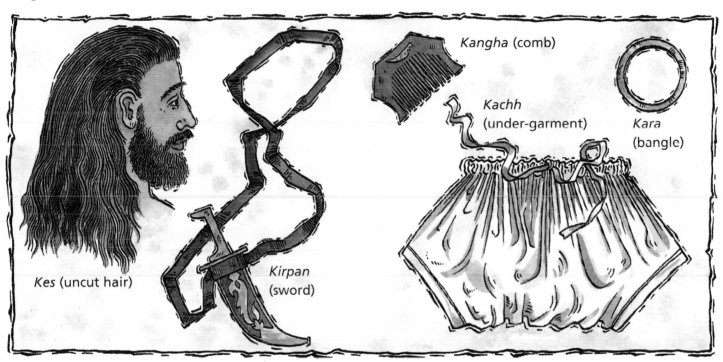

Kangha (comb)

Kachh (under-garment)

Kara (bangle)

Kes (uncut hair)

Kirpan (sword)

Turbans ▶

Sikh men wear turbans, although it is not one of the special signs members of the Khalsa were told to wear. The photograph shows many different-coloured turbans on sale in a turban shop.

WHAT HAPPENED AFTER THE LAST GURU DIED?

Guru Govind Singh died in 1708. Emperor Aurangzeb, the last great Mogul emperor, had died the year before. Fighting soon broke out in Panjab. Sikhs fought each other, as well as invaders from Afghanistan and Iran. The Harmandir in Amritsar (see page 28) was destroyed three times by the invaders. Each time, the Sikhs managed to drive back their attackers. They rebuilt the city and the Harmandir more beautifully than before.

▲ **Baba Dip Singh**
These people are visiting the spot beside the Harmandir in Amritsar where the Sikh hero Baba Dip Singh died. Baba Dip Singh was a scholar who took up a sword and went to fight the invaders. Some stories say that he carried on fighting even after his head was cut off.

◀ Maharaja Ranjit Singh

The picture on the left shows the court of Maharaja Ranjit Singh. The Maharaja was a great Sikh ruler who captured Lahore, the capital city of Panjab, when he was only 18. He gave huge amounts of money to the Harmandir, but he also gave money and gold to a Hindu temple and a devout Muslim. He said God had given him only one eye so that he should look at all religions equally.

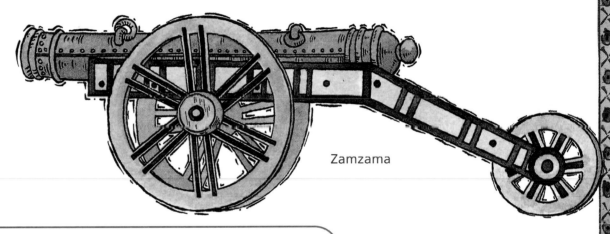

Zamzama

ZAMZAMA

Zamzama is a very large cannon, which belonged to Maharaja Ranjit Singh. It stands in Lahore, in the middle of the main route across India. Indians believe that whoever has Zamzama rules Panjab.

◀ The British Raj

The British ruled large areas of India in the early 1800s. When Ranjit Singh died there were wars between the Sikhs and the British. In 1849 the British took control of Panjab and ruled it until 1947. This period is called 'the Raj'. The photograph shows Sikh soldiers in the Indian army during the Raj.

WHAT IS THE SIKH HOLY BOOK LIKE?

The Sikh holy book was put together by Guru Arjan, the fifth Guru. It is called the *Sri Guru Granth Sahib*. There are no stories in the

book – it is a collection of poems, considered by Sikhs to be the word of God. They were written down by the first five Gurus, the ninth Guru and 35 other holy men from northern India.

▲ Looking after the Granth

Lamps with merging flames

The spirit of the Guru passed from one Guru to another, like two candle flames joining to become one. The same spirit of the Guru is in the holy book. This is why the book is treated with great respect. In this photograph the book is being put to bed for the night.

Guru Nanak's poem ▶

A poem describing Guru Nanak's basic belief about God appears on the first page of the Guru Granth Sahib (right). It says 'There is one God. He is the Truth. He is the Creator, and is without fear or hate. He is beyond time, is not born and does not die to be born again. He is known by His grace.'

 IDENTICAL PAGES

The Guru Granth Sahib has 1,430 pages. The same words always appear on the same page in every copy of the book. The handwritten book in the photograph is unique because it is so beautifully decorated.

Chaur

◀ The chaur

The *chaur*, or fan, is a symbol of royalty. It is waved over the Guru Granth Sahib while it is being read, as a sign of respect.

◀ Reading the Guru Granth Sahib

Any member of the congregation who wants to read from the Guru Granth Sahib may do so. The book is read aloud so that everyone in the *gurdwara* can hear. Some *gurdwaras* have sound systems so that the readings can be heard throughout the building. Each reader continues from the point where the previous reader finished.

WHAT DO SIKHS BELIEVE?

Sikhs believe that people should love God and obey Him as a child obeys a father. By praising God and following His laws, they will become closer to Him. Sikhs want to be united with God during their lives, rather than after death. There is a Sikh saying that sets out how people should live: 'Meditate on [think carefully about] the Name of God, earn an honest living and share what you have with others.'

Living a good life ▶

This Sikh woman is a doctor. Helping other people is important to Sikhs. They believe it is important to earn a living by working hard, and they think it is bad to beg.

The Name ▼

The words shown below are written in Gurmurkhi, the language of the Guru Granth Sahib. They are names for God. Many Sikhs like to say them over and over again because it helps them to feel close to God.

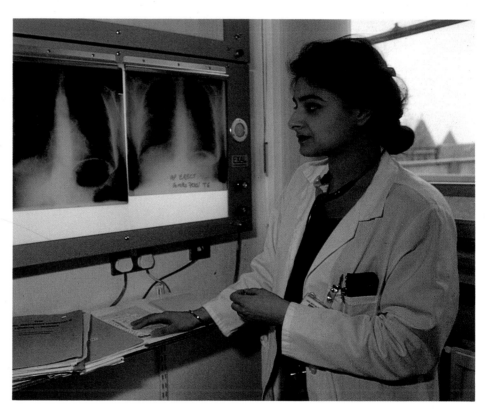

ਸਤਿਨਾਮੁ

Satnam – 'True Name'

ਵਾਹਿਗੁਰੂ

Wahiguru – 'Wonderful Lord'

One God ▶

This symbol appears at the beginning of every poem in the Guru Granth Sahib. It means 'There is one God.'

Ik Oankar

 SACRED WRITING

Sikhs never draw pictures of God but they are allowed to write His name. For this reason they always treat paper with writing on it very respectfully, in case the name of God appears on it.

Sharing with others ▶

The Sikhs in the photograph on the right are handing out drinks to people passing by their home. Some of the passers by are taking part in a procession to mark Guru Nanak's birthday but everyone is welcome to take a drink, whether they are Sikhs or not. Sikhs believe it is important to share whatever they have with others.

Mala – 'necklace'

▲ Serving the community

Being part of the community means helping at the gurdwara. This can involve everything from cleaning the building to looking after people's shoes at the entrance. The men in the photograph above are cleaning pots and pans with sand, after a meal at a *gurdwara* in India.

The *mala* ▲

Some Sikhs use a *mala* to help them concentrate on their prayers. The Sikh Gurus teach that prayer and meditation in God's name are the highest actions or deeds.

HOW DO SIKHS WORSHIP?

There is a regular service held at the *gurdwara* called Diwan. The Guru Granth Sahib is opened and the musicians sing *kirtan* (hymns). Members of the congregation might give a talk, tell a story or explain one of the Gurus' poems. The service can last all day and at the end everyone is offered a sweet food called *karah prasad*.

◀ Prayer book

This man is reading his daily prayers. There are prayers that are read in the morning, prayers to read during the day and prayers to read at bedtime.

The prayers are all from the Guru Granth Sahib but a Guru Granth Sahib cannot be used for everyday reading. People use a small prayer book like the one in the photograph.

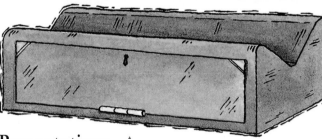

Collection box

Presentations ▲

People bring gifts of food, milk or money to the *gurdwara*. The gifts are placed in front of the Guru Granth Sahib. The food and milk is then taken to the Guru's kitchen, which is called the *langar*, where it is used to make the shared meal.

Removing shoes ▼

Sikhs take off their shoes before they approach the Guru Granth Sahib. Some Sikhs also wash their feet.

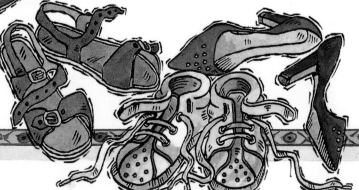

Ardas ▲

Every ritual begins and ends with a prayer called *ardas*. Worshippers remember the Gurus and important events that happened in their faith in the past. They pray for the Sikh community and for all people. They can also pray especially for people who need help and comfort.

READING

On special occasions such as a festival, the entire Guru Granth Sahib is read by a team of readers. This unbroken reading is called *akhand path* and it takes 48 hours.

◄ Bowing

When people enter the *gurdwara* they bow towards the Guru Granth Sahib, to show respect. They never turn their back on the holy book and never point their feet towards it when they are sitting down.

WHERE DO SIKHS WORSHIP?

Sikhs can worship anywhere. The presence of the Guru Granth Sahib is what makes a place special. Schools, halls, people's homes and even disused cinemas are used if there is no specially built *gurdwara* nearby. However, the building must be clean, free from meat or alcohol and the holy book must always be placed on a throne with a canopy over it.

Nishan Sahib

▲ *Gurdwara*

This *gurdwara* was built in Australia in the mid-1990s by the local Sikh community. The word 'gurdwara' means 'a doorway to the Guru' because it is a place that allows people to move closer to God.

Nishan Sahib ▶

The Nishan Sahib is the flag that flies outside the *gurdwara*. The flag and the cloth that is wrapped around the flagpole are orange. The *khanda*, the Sikh emblem, is dark blue. A double-edged sword tops the flagpole.

SEEING GOD'S CREATION

Sikhs believe that the best way to understand God is through seeing His creation. This is why they think it is important to worship God wherever they are.

Rumalas ►

Rumalas are beautiful embroidered cloths that are draped around the Guru Granth Sahib. They cover the holy book when no one is reading from it.

Rumala

Worship at home ▲

Most people do not have enough space in their home to keep a Guru Granth Sahib there all the time. On special occasions the holy book is brought to their home for an unbroken reading (*akhand path*). This might take place to mark a family event such as the birth of a baby, a wedding or a funeral.

Inside the *gurdwara* ►

The *gurdwara* is set out like the court of an Indian king. The Guru Granth Sahib is at the front on its throne. The musicians sit on one side of the holy book and the *karah prasad* is kept on the other side. The congregation (*sangat*) sits on the floor. Men sit on one side of the room and women on the other, although this is a social custom and not for any special religious reason.

WHAT IS THE HARMANDIR?

The Harmandir Sahib stands in the centre of a pool in Amritsar. Its name means 'God's temple'. It is also known as the Darbar Sahib (God's court), and as the Golden Temple, because the top of the building is decorated with pure gold. Although Sikhs do not go on pilgrimages they do enjoy visiting the beautiful temple with its wonderful atmosphere. The temple has an entrance on each side, to show that people from all directions are welcome to enter.

The building of the temple ▲

The pool that surrounds the temple was actually built first, on the orders of Guru Ram Das, the fourth Guru. The first temple was built by Guru Arjan in 1588 but was demolished three times by invaders in the 1700s. The present temple was built in 1788 and most of the gold that was used to decorate it was a gift from Maharaja Ranjit Singh.

◀ The main entrance

This intricately decorated gold panel is above the main door. The writing on it is a quotation from Guru Nanak's description of God. It also reminds worshippers of the help that Maharaja Ranjit Singh gave to the temple.

 GOLD

The Harmandir is covered with gilded copper and decorated with gold. It is cleaned with washing powder and polished energetically to make it shine.

Decoration ▼

Hindu and Muslim artists, as well as Sikhs, worked on the decorations inside the Harmandir. Many of the decorations show plants and animals, like the ones in the drawings below.

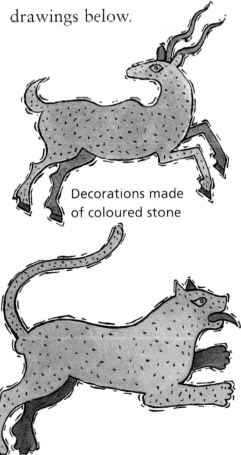

Decorations made of coloured stone

Bathing ▲

These Sikhs are bathing in the pool at Amritsar. According to some stories, people who bathe in the waters there will live for ever.

HOW DO SIKH FAMILIES LIVE?

Family life is important to Sikhs. It is traditional for a woman to go to live with her new husband's family when she marries. The whole family works together on the farm or in business, eats together, and shares the costs of running the home. Large family groups like this are known as extended families. Eventually the family becomes too big to live together and it splits into smaller groups.

Family groups ▶

Sikhs do not marry their relatives or people from their family village, so they usually have relatives spread over a large area. The family in the photograph is from Amritsar but they have relatives in other towns in India and in Britain.

Father's side			Mother's side
Nackarpardada Nackarpardadi	—	Great great grandparents —	Nackarparnana Nackarparnani
Pardada Pardadi	—	Great grandparents —	Parnana Parnani
Dada (Grandfather)		Grandparents	Nana (Grandfather)
Dadi (Grandmother)			Nani (Grandmother)

Parents Uncles Aunts Parents' cousins

You Brothers Sisters Cousins

Children

Son's children			Daughter's children
Potra (Boy) Potri (Girl)	—	Grandchild —	Dotra (boy) Dotri (girl)
Parpotra Parpotri	—	Great grandchild —	Pardotra Pardotri
Nackarparpotra Nackarparpotri	—	Great great grandchild —	Nackarpardotra Nackarpardotri

RELATIONSHIPS

Relatives are given different titles depending on whether they are on the mother's side of the family or the father's side. You can see some of the titles in the family tree on the left.

Getting together ▶

Sikhs enjoy getting together with members of their extended families and with other Sikhs. They often arrange parties or outings. This group is enjoying a day out at the British seaside resort of Blackpool.

◀ Small families

In countries such as Canada, Britain and the USA, it is more common for Sikhs to live in small families, like the one in the photograph on the left. Few houses are big enough for large extended families.

Sport and games ▼

Many Sikhs love sport, especially team sports such as cricket and hockey. They also enjoy games, such as *carrom*, a traditional Indian game. The first player to flick all their counters and then the Queen into a pocket wins.

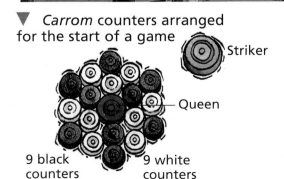

▼ *Carrom* counters arranged for the start of a game

Striker

Queen

9 black counters

9 white counters

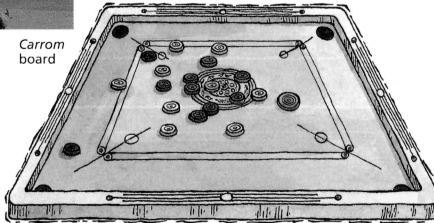

Carrom board

WHAT ARE THE MOST IMPORTANT TIMES IN A SIKH'S LIFE?

Marriage is a very special event for Sikhs. Many traditional rituals take place before the wedding itself, to bring the two families together. Joining the Khalsa is another important occasion. Some Sikhs hold a ceremony called taking *pahul* to mark the event. The new members of the Khalsa are given a sweet drink called *amrit* and *amrit* is also sprinkled over them. This is the ritual that was used when Guru Govind Singh became a member of the Khalsa.

Henna patterns ▼

One old wedding tradition is to paint patterns on the bride's hands and feet with a red dye called henna.

Patterns on a bride's hand

▲ The wedding ceremony

The bride and groom in the photograph are walking around the Guru Granth Sahib with their scarves tied together. As they walk, a hymn about marriage by Guru Ram Das is sung. When they have circled the holy book four times, they become husband and wife.

Veil and jewellery ▼ ▶

Traditionally the bridegroom leaves home wearing a veil of red material and tinsel. The bride wears red and white bangles and gold jewellery.

A special ornament hangs from her wrist.

Bridegroom's veil

Bride's ornaments

Bride's bangles

Degree ceremony ▼

This woman has completed her university studies and received her degree. Education is very important to Sikhs.

A new baby ▼

Some people read a prayer by Guru Nanak into a new baby's ear. They go to the *gurdwara* for a blessing. The baby is given a taste of *amrit* and some *amrit* is sprinkled over it. Many Sikhs choose their baby's name by opening the Guru Granth Sahib and picking a name that begins with the first letter on the page.

WHAT ARE THE SIKH FESTIVALS?

Sikhs have two kinds of festival. *Gurpurbs* are the anniversaries of the births and deaths of the ten Gurus. Guru Nanak's birthday is especially popular. Many Sikhs also like to mark the deaths of Guru Teg Bahadar and Guru Arjan because these Gurus died defending their faith. The other kind of festival is a *mela* – a traditional fair.

Nishan Sahib

▲ Vaisakhi

Vaisakhi, on 13 April, marks the anniversary of the founding of the Khalsa. The flagpole at the *gurdwara* is taken down at this *mela*. The old wrappings are taken off and the pole is washed in yoghurt to purify it. In the photograph above, the congregation is raising the flagpole in its clean wrappings. A new Nishan Sahib will fly from the top.

◀ Diwali

Diwali is celebrated by Sikhs and Hindus, although the Sikh Diwali story is different from the Hindu version. Children light candles and lamps and receive presents. The Harmandir Sahib in Amritsar is lit up for the festival.

THE SIKH STORY OF DIWALI

Guru Hargovind was about to be released from prison by the Emperor. He asked if the other prisoners could be freed too. The Emperor said that he would free the prisoners who could squeeze through a narrow passage while holding on to the Guru's clothes. The Guru wore a cloak with long tassels on the end and 52 men were able to hold on to it and go free.

Guru Nanak's birthday ▶

The photograph on the right shows a procession that is taking place on Guru Nanak's birthday. Five men representing the Five Beloved Ones who founded the Khalsa lead the procession. Other people carry flags and banners. The Guru Granth Sahib is carried on a decorated float or lorry.

WHY IS EATING TOGETHER IMPORTANT?

People in India used to be divided into different social groups, or castes. They did not mix with or marry members of other castes. Guru Nanak set up the Guru's kitchen to show that he did not accept the caste system. Everyone cooked, served food and ate together. Eating together is still important for Sikhs. The kitchen at the *gurdwara* and the food that is cooked there are both called the *langar*.

◄ Karah prasad

Karah prasad is special food that is given out in the prayer hall, instead of in the *langar*. While it is being cooked, some special verses by Guru Govind Singh are said over it and it is stirred with a sword. The man in the photograph is cutting the *karah prasad* with a *kirpan*.

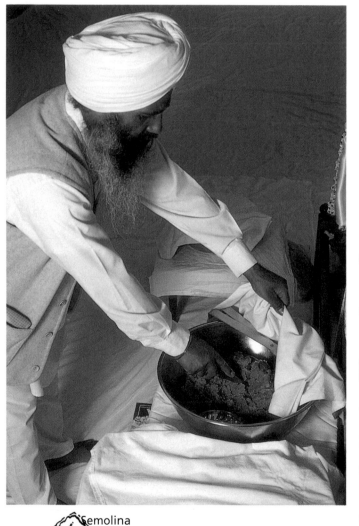

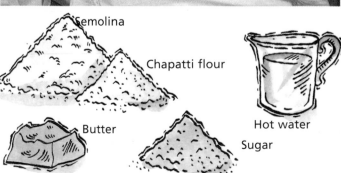

Semolina

Chapatti flour

Butter

Sugar

Hot water

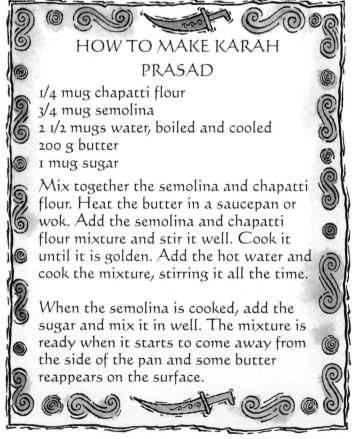

HOW TO MAKE KARAH PRASAD

1/4 mug chapatti flour
3/4 mug semolina
2 1/2 mugs water, boiled and cooled
200 g butter
1 mug sugar

Mix together the semolina and chapatti flour. Heat the butter in a saucepan or wok. Add the semolina and chapatti flour mixture and stir it well. Cook it until it is golden. Add the hot water and cook the mixture, stirring it all the time.

When the semolina is cooked, add the sugar and mix it in well. The mixture is ready when it starts to come away from the side of the pan and some butter reappears on the surface.

Pangat ▶

The photograph on the right shows people giving out food in the *langar*. The people eating always sit in lines, so that no one seems to be more important than anyone else. This is called *pangat*. In hot countries they sit on the ground and might eat off leaves instead of plates. In Western countries they set out lines of tables and chairs.

◀ Cooking in the *gurdwara*

Any Sikh can bring food to the *gurdwara*, prepare it and serve it. However, as the photograph on the left shows, the pots are so big that strong arms are needed for stirring! Cooking food is a way of performing *seva*, or service to the community.

ARE THE SIKHS GREAT TRAVELLERS?

People who live in the Panjab have travelled widely since ancient times. The routes used by traders travelling between Europe and China and between India and Central Asia passed through or close to  Panjab. The Gurus were great travellers. Guru Nanak travelled as far as Baghdad in present-day Iraq and to the Muslim holy city of Makkah, in Saudi Arabia.

▲ Guru Nanak's travels

Many stories are told about Guru Nanak's travels. In these adventures the Guru usually meets evil people or creatures. The picture above, for example, shows a demon who is about to cook the Guru's friend, Mardana. By the end of the story the evil ones are so impressed by Guru Nanak's teaching that they become Sikhs.

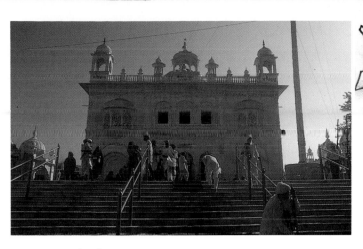

▲ Nanded

The photograph above shows the *gurdwara* at Nanded. This is where Guru Govind Singh died. You can see where Nanded is on the map on the right. Other gurus travelled as far as eastern India.

JATHEDARS

Jathedars are paid officials who are in charge of the Takhats. They are sometimes described as 'high priests' but there are no priests in the Sikh religion.

The five Takhats ▲

The map above shows where the five Takhats or Sikh 'thrones' can be found. Guru Hargovind built the first one, the Akal Takhat, as his court in Amritsar. The others are linked to events in the life of Guru Govind Singh. He was born in Patna and died at Nanded. The Khalsa was founded at Keshgarh. Damdama Sahib is the place where the final Guru Granth Sahib was dictated.

Community projects ▶

The Sikhs in the photograph are helping with a building project. Sikhs think it is important to work together to carry out jobs like this. Often, whole buildings are put up or repaired by volunteers. One of the most popular jobs is cleaning out the pool at Amritsar.

DO SIKHS ENJOY MUSIC AND DANCE?

Each poem in the Guru Granth Sahib is set to music. This suggests that the Gurus understood music and thought it was important. Traditional Indian music is not written down. It is based around tunes called *ragas*, which have about five or seven notes. There are thirty-one different *ragas* in the Guru Granth Sahib.

Today many young Sikhs prefer Western pop music and the music from Indian films to traditional Indian music.

▲ Music in a *gurdwara*

Skilled musicians called Ragis travel from one *gurdwara* to another. They work in groups of three. One plays a drum or drums. Another plays a harmonium. The third leads the singing. The music is kept simple so that everyone can join in. In most *gurdwaras* young people are encouraged to learn to play instruments and join in the services, like the children in this photograph.

RAGAS

Ragas have different moods – they can be happy, sad or peaceful. There are also *ragas* that are suitable for different seasons or times of day.

◄ Bhangra dancing

Bhangra dancing is a Punjabi tradition that is performed at harvest time. Farmers put on colourful clothes and tie bells around their ankles. Some men beat drums and others circle, stamping their feet and clapping their hands. The dance gets faster and noisier until everyone is exhausted.

Drums ▼

Tabla drums are struck on the top while *dholaks* are struck at both ends. Drummers use drumsticks to play the larger ones but strike smaller ones with their hands.

Dholak

◄ Pop music

Indian and Western music have influenced each other. '*Bhangra* beat' is a mixture of traditional *Bhangra* music and disco music that is very popular. Some young Sikhs are expert rappers.

DO SIKHS LIKE STORIES?

Sikhs love stories, especially stories with a moral. For example, one

story tells the tale of two brothers, who were shown that it was easy to break a single stick but very difficult to break a bundle of sticks. This taught them that they were stronger together than apart, so they should work together. Sikhs also enjoy stories about famous and holy men. Love stories, like the tale of Hir and Ranjha retold below, are popular stories enjoyed by all Indians and Pakistanis.

▲ The Guru's palm print

Once, Guru Nanak was travelling with his friend Mardana. Mardana was very thirsty, so the Guru sent him to ask a holy man for some water from his well. Three times the holy man refused, and told Guru Nanak to give water to his friend himself. Guru Nanak struck the ground with his staff and water sprang up. Now the holy man found that his own water supply had dried up. In a rage he threw a boulder at the Guru. Guru Nanak stopped it with his hand and his handprint can still be seen on the rock to this day.

The story of Hir and Ranjha

Once there was a young man called Ranjha, the youngest in his family, who loved to play the flute. One day he heard about a beautiful woman called Hir. He became determined to find her and win her love.

Ranjha's journey was a difficult one but he was blessed by five holy men and eventually he came to the place where Hir lived. He told the beautiful woman his story and played his enchanting music. She quickly fell in love with him.

Hir found Ranjha a job caring for the villagers' cattle. In the afternoons they would meet and talk of love. But Hir's uncle saw them together and told her parents. They were furious. They decided to marry Hir at once to the man she had been promised to since she was a child. Hir wept as they took her away. Ranjha went up into the mountains and became a holy man.

HIDDEN MEANINGS

Many people believe that stories like the tale of Hir and Ranjha have hidden meanings. The lovers represent God and the human soul. The two always become separated and they suffer dreadfully. Religious teachers say that a person has to love God as strongly as the lovers love each other in order to know Him properly.

After the marriage, a flute-playing healer came to the area where Hir lived. Hir realized at once that it was Ranjha. She pretended to have been bitten by a snake and sent for the healer. As soon as they were alone they ran into each other's arms and made a plan to run away together.

Hir's husband tried to get her back, but a court said that the marriage was not lawful because Hir had never agreed to it. Hir was free to marry Ranjha at last.

Ranjha left Hir at her parents' home while he went to invite his relatives to the wedding. Hir's parents thought she had brought shame on them, because everyone had seen her leave home to get married and now she was getting married again. One day they gave her a drink containing poison and she fell to the ground, calling Ranjha's name with her dying breath.

Ranjha heard something was wrong and hurried back to Hir's home – too late. Heartbroken, he fell dead upon Hir's grave.

▲ Children reading

In the past, story tellers used to go from village to village, telling tales about heroes, kings and monsters. They also told stories about the Gurus and holy men from other religions. Today, children enjoy reading the same stories in picture books and comics and on television.

GLOSSARY

Akal Takhat The first of the Sikh 'thrones', built by Guru Hargovind beside the Harmandir at Amritsar between 1606 and 1609. From this building he dealt out justice and carried out other non-religious work.

Amrit A sweet drink, used to initiate Sikhs into the Khalsa.

Amritsar The city in Panjab in north-west India which was built by the Sikh Gurus. The name means 'the pool of nectar' (from *amrit* meaning nectar and *sar* meaning pool).

Guru Guru has several meanings, including God as people can know him, and the voice of our conscience. The human Gurus were teachers and leaders.

Guru Granth Sahib The Sikh holy book.

Harmandir Sahib The temple in Amritsar, also known as the Golden Temple and the Darbar Sahib.

Harmonium A keyboard instrument.

Karah prasad Sweet food given out at the end of the service in the prayer hall of the *gurdwara*.

Moguls The people who invaded India in the sixteenth century and ruled it for two hundred years.

Sari A dress made from a single piece of material, folded around the body.

Turban A long piece of cloth folded around the head.

Vaisakhi The anniversary of the founding of the Khalsa.

INDEX